LIVE YOUR BEST LIFE

BY WRITING YOUR OWN EULOGY

Includes

SAMPLE EULOGY TO-BE, TEMPLATES
AND REVERSE ENGINEER HOW TO's

Mimi's Guardian Angel
aka Mimi Emmanuel, friends & family

Live Your Best Life by Writing Your Own Eulogy
Includes Sample Eulogy To-Be, Templates and Reverse Engineer How-To's
By Mimi's Guardian Angel (aka Mimi Emmanuel, friends, & family)

DISCLAIMER –
The word eulogy is a common word. The word 'eulogy-to-be' is a concession we had to make because certain family members became quite traumatised when the subject of writing a eulogy popped up.
A 'eulogy' is a celebration of someone's life in words *after* this person has died. These words are spoken about people when they can no longer participate in the flesh, talk back, or prepare a come-back.
A 'eulogy-to-be' is a write-up for the purpose of getting perspective on life so that we can adjust course if necessary, and celebrate life every single day and not miss out on our own final party.
A 'eulogy-to-be' is a tried and tested method to help people get back on track. As in: *What would you like people to say about you after you die? Now go and create that.*

ISBN – 9781975956059
Another Mosaic House publication.
The author can be contacted at www.mimiemmanuel.com
Po Box 25 Noosa, Qld 4567, Australia

All rights reserved – ©2017 myemmanuel.
The content, formatting and design may not in any way be emulated, reproduced, duplicated, or copied in any manner without prior written permission from the publisher.

Created in the Commonwealth of Australia
Printed and distributed in the United States of America
Cover design by SunnyEdesign and Mimi
Formatting by SunnyEdesign
Editing by Elaine Roughton

Contents

THANK YOU 1

ABOUT MIMI 3

ABOUT THIS BOOK 5

INTRO 9

    Why write your own eulogy to be? 9

        Eulogy versus eulogy-to-be 9

        How To Live Your Best Life Ever? 11

        Celebrate your life 13

EULOGY-TO-BE FOR MIMI EMMANUEL 19

    Childhood/early life 19

    Medical emergencies 21

    Mimi's Mission 21

    Fun times 22

    Joys of her life 23

    Failures 23

        Model 24

        Author 24

        Medical 24

        Entrepreneur 24

        Gardener 25

    Friendships and other things 25

        Award Winning Series Letters to my Godchild 26

        Health restored 26

        Mimi's favourites 27

        Breath of fresh air 28

LYRICAL POEM BY CRYSTAL 29

    The secret of reverse engineering 31

Why and how write your own eulogy-to-be?		33
Live forever		36
AFTERWORD		41
YOUR STORY IS YOUR LEGACY		45
TEMPLATE FOR EULOGY-TO-BE		49
1.	Introduction	50
2.	Childhood	50
3.	Schooling and Education	51
4.	Work and Professional	51
5.	Family and Marriage	52
6.	Voluntary work, hobbies, and sport	52
8.	Look around you	53
9.	For Inspiration	54
10.	Reflections, Dreams, Hopes	54
11.	Go for it! Make it happen!	55
NOTES		57

THANK YOU

Thank you to some of the best Guardian Angels that I know; John, Kathryn, Karin, Karina, Syed, Robyn, Colleen, Elizabeth, Mutti, Andrew, Angie, Meera, Stacey, Sunny, Elaine, Celine, Gerda, Olivia, Amanda, Jan, Ann, Greg, Richard, Ben and Kim; I love you!

ABOUT MIMI

My Guardian Angel told me to go and 'help some folk.'

Nice one that... when you're on your back in a dark room and can only stand up for minutes at a time. I had no connection to the outside world either, other than the occasional doctor (home) visit, who insisted on keeping me, 'comfortable.'

I quietly raged about this. Wouldn't have been surprised if smoke plumes were emanating from the top of my head.

'Help some folk.' Righto.

Eventually I decided to write about my experiences. We're now six books later and you can find these on www.mimiemmanuel.com and Amazon.

You can download your free template to write your own eulogy-to-be from www.mimiemmanuel.com/downloads/template-for-eulogy-to-be

ABOUT THIS BOOK

What do Amazon customers say about this book?

⭐⭐⭐⭐⭐ **Great Reminders!**

This fun little book is full of important reminders of why it is so important to live life on purpose. It is never too late to redirect. Love the visual the author created of the singed feathers of her guardian angel!
By Kim Diede on September 2, 2017

⭐⭐⭐⭐⭐ ***A MUST HAVE IN EVERYONE'S SPECIAL COLLECTION OF BOOKS!***

I found sweetness, beauty, hope, joy and love on every page of this short and happy book.
I paused, reflected and thought about my life as I live it on a daily basis and get to ask myself what my eulogy would be.
This is one of those special books that anyone should have.
By Elsa Mendoza on September 5, 2017

★★★★★ THIS DELIGHTFUL READ IS THE PERFECT PRESCRIPTION FOR 'GETTING IT RIGHT - NOW.'

I thank God above for fresh lingerie and Bonus Moments! This delightful read is the perfect prescription for 'getting it right - now.' Don't wait until later to figure out what your very best life, joy and happiness are meant to be. Mimi offers a fantastic template to help you think about what really matters, here and now. My only regret is the author lives on the other side of the world and isn't available to jaunt around with. Because if she was I'd be at her house every day soaking up her enthusiasm. I look forward to more from Ms. Emmanuelle. By Amazon Customer on September 5, 2017

★★★★★ AN INSPIRING READ WITH A PRACTICAL APPLICATION

If you've wondered what you're meant to be doing with your life, take stock and read this! What a great idea for getting your life back on track.. how to reverse engineer your life. Love it! By Amazon Customer on September 4, 2017

⭐⭐⭐⭐⭐ *WHAT A GREAT WAY TO WALK THROUGH LIFE!*

What a great way to walk through life! Mimi is thought provoking and engaging. She gets us thinking about what kind of legacy we leave to this world. I highly recommend this book! By Amazon Customer on September 4, 2017

INTRO

*"Your life doesn't just 'happen.'
Whether you know it or not, it is carefully designed by you."*
Dr. R. Covey, author

Why write your own eulogy-to-be?

Why on earth would anyone ever want to write their own eulogy-to-be? Well, sometimes life just sucks, and then consequently your eulogy would suck too. Double whammy.

Mimi decided to make her life follow her eulogy-to-be. Yes, wrap your mind around that! It's a work in progress.

Eulogy versus eulogy-to-be
The word eulogy-to-be is a concession we had to make because certain family members became quite traumatised when the subject of writing a eulogy popped up.

I used to think that a eulogy is a celebration of someone's life in words *after* this person has died. With words spoken about people when they can no longer participate in the flesh, talk back, or prepare a come-back.

However, some writers agree that eulogies are not exclusive for funeral services.

> *A eulogy can also be used to praise a person who has achieved a milestone, who has recently retired from years of service, or who has surpassed a great obstacle in his or her life. Remember that a eulogy is a speech that is meant to deliver praise and to celebrate all the good things in the life of a person. Therefore, although it is mostly associated with the passing of a loved one, a eulogy may also be a congratulatory speech for those who are still living.*

The above is quoted from *Eulogy Writing For Beginners: How To Write The Perfect Eulogy* by Dianne Michelle. Her book also goes into detail about the different funeral traditions for different religions.

A eulogy-to-be is a write-up for the purpose of getting perspective on life so that we can adjust course if necessary, and celebrate life every single day and not miss out on our own final party. See urban dictionary for a spot-on definition www.urbandictionary.com/define.php?term=eulogy-to-be

TOP DEFINITION

eulogy-to-be

A 'eulogy-to-be' is a write-up for the purpose of getting perspective on <u>life</u> so that we can adjust course if necessary, and celebrate life every <u>single</u> day, and not miss out on our own final <u>party</u>.

<u>One</u> of the finer pleasures in life is to have <u>one's</u> guardian angel create a eulogy-to-be for their <u>charge</u>, to keep them on <u>track</u>.

As in, "Is this how you would like to be remembered?"

How To Live Your Best Life Ever?

If you wonder where to go next, what step to take first, think no more! Reverse engineer your life!

Imagine how you would like to be remembered and then make it happen.

The following is what happened to Mimi.

The events leading up to Mimi's eulogy-to-be

Imagine a full moon on the 20th of July 2008. Two people die in a motor vehicle accident in a small coastal town in Queensland, Australia.

Surrounded by death and physicians' heroic efforts to save lives and limbs, Mimi thought about her lingerie drawer at home. She should have thrown that underwear out years ago. As she was drifting in and out of consciousness she tried to alert one of her daughters to this very important oversight. She couldn't even lift her finger. Oh no, what if she weren't able to make it back home, ever, and strangers would open her smalls drawer?

Praise the Lord, Mimi made it back home and prioritised the purchase of fresh lingerie, and with the help of her daughters put order to her drawers, paperwork, and financial affairs.

That fatal event on the Esplanade of their new town, combined with Mimi's medical emergency, caused Mimi to contemplate her life, and nearly a decade ago now, to write her eulogy-to-be. She hated what her life had become. One of her main concerns when death was threatening was her lingerie drawer? Like, really? Where to go from here? At mid-life, her life story/legacy was pretty much set in stone... or was it?

Confined to bed, in the year 2008 Mimi looked at the eulogy-to-be she just wrote and utterly despised and rejected it. She didn't just get out a red marker, but tore up the pieces of paper and rewrote her eulogy-to-be.

Now she had something to live up to. That same day she resolved to live according to her newly rewritten eulogy-to-be. The one that she would be proud to have read out at her funeral. And that very day, she took the first step toward making that her reality.

Celebrate your life

What is a eulogy? A eulogy is nothing other than a celebration of someone's life. Why wait with celebrating your life till you're gone? This doesn't make any sense at all.

Research has shown again and again that people who fail to plan, actually plan to fail. And the only things that matter in the end are not what we accomplish in life but how we made others feel in the process. And did we love creating our legacy or hate every moment of it?

It matters hugely that we're aligned with our unique task in life. What is our mission? What were we uniquely born to accomplish? This obviously will be different for all of us, and can be several things which may change over a lifetime.

Whilst confined to bed recuperating, Mimi contemplated all these things and realised that our life story creates our legacy. Whilst previously she may have lived rather unconsciously, after her mishaps, she decided to intentionally make her legacy the best it can be.

After re-arranging her smalls drawer, Mimi changed her perception of her reality, from a potential mourning of death to a conscious decision to celebrate life daily.

Fast forward nine years and it is January 2017. Mimi, with the help of her daughters, has created MOSAIC HOUSE, and has also become an international bestselling author.

All this came about because of her near-death experience. As an exercise, she wrote her eulogy-to-be, hated what she saw, tore it up, rewrote it and took the first few steps towards achieving her goals.

Every so often Mimi reflects on her life and adjusts course if necessary. Her following eulogy-to-be is her latest update and she intends to outlive this eulogy-to-be also.

Mimi discovered that there is something miraculous about the process of writing down and sharing your dreams and aspirations. *HE created the Heaven and the Earth by the breath of HIS mouth, and we were made in HIS image*. There is a lesson in there somewhere. See NOTES for this link.

> YOURSTORYOURLEGACY
>
> There is something miraculous about sharing your dreams & aspirations with the Universe
>
> Angels listen in
>
> © www.mimiemmanuel.com

EULOGY-TO-BE FOR MIMI EMMANUEL

Hi there. Mimi's moving on means that I'm temporarily out of a job. How so? Well, as Mimi's Guardian Angel, this assignment concluded when I passed her over to her family.

The brownie points I accrued for keeping her going for 10 decades mean that I can pick wherever I want to go for my holidays. The Bahamas, Fiji, or any of the heavenly places; the sky literally is the limit here.

Childhood/early life
What can I say about Mimi, or Kikkie, as she was known in her youth? The middle daughter of Charles and Peggi Sketch-Fafie, born in Australia and raised in Europe, she was not an easy one to keep in this earthly realm. The opposition launched savage attacks on the mother of Georgie and Crystal and Godmother of Lewis, throughout her life. She defended with dignity and calm, always checking in with Headquarters to make sure that she was following the Guidelines and stuck with the rules.

Born in Sydney, Australia, she crossed the equator as a baby and was baptised 'little prawn' by Neptune; a name she effortlessly lived up to.

Mimi's parents owned a beach kiosk in Hoek van Holland, and I fondly recall those years of beachcombing and wind surfing fun. She was a favourite of the lifesavers, and the times she was frolicking with them in the waves were about the only times that I got to chill out too.

We had quite a few close calls. Throughout her earlier years Mimi spent many hours on the road in Europe as well as Australia for her job modelling and promoting, and this is where we fended off numerous attacks. Despite being an excellent driver, Mimi's cars slipped and slid on icy roads, rainy and oily roads, as well as on snow and gravel. Her cars were bumped from behind a number of times. Some were totalled. She nearly ended up in a ravine, and even landed amid a copse of trees on one occasion. Any of these events could have been her last on this earth, but her faith in our Helpers above and my wings helped us through.

If you remember seeing white feathers tumbling down from Heaven, these may very well have been mine, whilst on duty for Mimi Emmanuel.

Medical emergencies
Eventually the opposition changed tack, and she endured a number of attempts on her life through medical emergencies. The last major one landed her in the emergency room in the hospital with an inoperable ruptured appendix and septicemia, whilst intolerant to antibiotics. Mimi's daughters became her gatekeepers. Their strong love for their mother was never more apparent than when they joined me, and did not leave her side for more than a year, whilst constantly appealing to the Big Boss to keep Mum with us for some time to come. Our request was granted.

Mimi's Mission
Battle scarred and temporarily immobilized after surviving this major life-threatening medical emergency, Mimi took a stand. 'Every minute has become a bonus minute,' she said. 'From now on, my seconds and my minutes will be dedicated to my Saviour.'
She realised that all of us have been given unique tasks in life.

When Mimi's efforts to secure a permanent home for her and her daughters failed, she founded, with the help of her daughters, MOSAIC HOUSE. **M**imi's **O**riginal **S**cripture **& I**nspirational **C**ard House. Her Scripture and Inspirational Cards are treasured by her customers. Within a year her books reached

#1 bestseller status in more than 40 categories on Amazon. As a multiple bestselling author Mimi dedicated the rest of her life to helping others find the peace and joy that she herself experienced throughout her life because of her faith.

Fun times

I savour the times when we were sharing lunch, on Mimi's verandah, with her friends the butcher birds and her puppies Layla-Joy and Lilac-Delite. She loved basking in sunrises and sunsets. She enjoyed nothing more than hanging out with family and friends. She was a skilled stand-up paddle board surfer, and at middle age learned the extreme sport of slacklining. The whole neighbourhood knew Mimi from her jogs around the block with puppies in tow, her drum solos, saxophone tunes, and card game nights filled with squeals of laughter...

The memories of joining Mimi on her strolls along the shore line with her nearest and dearest still warm my heart. Mimi thrived on the loving relationship she had with her brothers and sisters.

Joys of her life

The biggest reward of her life was to put smiles on her children's faces. When they were little she'd scrounge coins from under her car seat for soft serve ice creams, and when they were older she saved up to teach them 'walking on water,' dancing, singing, archery, aikido, and horse riding.

Mimi raised her daughters to be the outstanding human beings they are today. Both happily married now, with a combined offspring of 11 grandchildren, and always ready to help anywhere this is needed, they will continue Mimi's Legacy and spread joy, love, and inspiration wherever they go as Custodians of Mosaic House. Mimi's daughters are an absolute credit to her. Always by her side, they referred to each other as besties. It is without a doubt that, together with her last partner, Mimi's children were the great loves of her life.

Failures

Mimi's successes came to her later in life and I'm sure that she would like you to know that for each success she experienced multiple failures.

Model
The day before her first modelling assignment, Mimi had a cigarette lighter that had been laying in the sun explode in her face. No permanent damage, but no eyebrows or hair fringe either, and plenty of blisters to bear testimony.

Author
She spent five years writing '*How Not To Raise Kids,*' but it took another twenty before it was finally published. Together with her children she created the book '*Jetties of Noosa,*' which was well received when exhibited at the local art gallery, but was unable to finish this project due to changing priorities and moving house.

Medical
Mimi was involved in the medical industry for many years and worked tremendously hard behind the scenes, as she set up one and managed three medical clinics. Due to burnout, she lost everything plus some.

Entrepreneur
She prepared to set up a 'Gossamer Empire' of delicate wildflowers and ornate two-metre-long gorgeous-looking weeds to be delivered to Noosa's finest hotels and resorts. Instead she ended up in bed covered in hives and

scratches after her field trip of collecting 'stock.'

Mimi never did anything half-heartedly; even to say wholeheartedly wouldn't do her justice.

Gardener
She and her ventures have fallen over more times than the pins in any bowling alley.

She loved gardening and growing her own veggies and edible flowers. The local wildlife liked the produce even more than she did. She was happy to grow surplus and share, but found it near impossible to compete with horse and pony hooves and appetite. She discovered at least one hundred ways of 'How *Not* To Defeat Bush Rats and Other Wildlife that eats homegrown flowers and vegetables.'

What defined Mimi was not her failures and disappointments in life, but her tenacity, optimism, and great faith.
She ended up growing a magnificent herb garden *inside* her house.

Friendships and other things

Mimi hugely valued her friends and would like you to know how much she cherished your friendship. It is too long a list to include here, but if you had regular contact with Mimi, be assured that she counted you amongst her friends and spoke about you often with love and appreciation.

All Mimi's mates remember her legendary root vegetable soup (see recipe in the NOTES) with toast and many a Grey Nomad fondly recalls the sessions shared with her as she helped them create and publish their best possible Legacy.

Award Winning Series Letters to my Godchild

Mimi hated insincerity and hypocrisy, and she will also be remembered for her award-winning series *'Letters to My Godchild.'* Millions of Godparents sit down every day and relish the time they spend with their Godchildren reading from Mimi's Letters. Her letters are unique in that they allow Grand- and Godparents to have input in the faith life of their Grand- and Godchildren, giving a balanced view, which is a precious gift in today's world.

I was never more excited than when I saw these fine books distributed all around the world, significantly lightening the load of many a Guardian Angel.

Health restored

We've raised numerous toasts to celebrate victories and in gratitude to the Good Forces who helped her and myself through many struggles and battles. My tattered and scorched feathers are a testimony to my zeal in guarding Mimi. Injured as she may have become over time, due to the incessant attacks on her health and wellbeing, her faith has been solid and unwavering throughout. Her health, thankfully, was restored to her completely and was much better in her later years than in her earlier life.

Mimi's loyalty for everyone she knew was fierce; she loved passionately and without reservations. Her dedication to her children and partner was steadfast and her devotion to her Saviour strong and undeniable. She casually brushed off death threats that came her way because of her belief.

Mimi's favourites
Mimi had a special affinity with birds. Wounded and exhausted birds often sought shelter with her. Her favourite musics was the daily duets of butcher birds and other feathered friends, accompanied by the background symphony of waves breaking on the shoreline.

Mimi brushed her teeth with charcoal (try it), she loved celebrations with ice creams on the beach, her favourite drink was Zwarte Kip advokaat with cream, she giggled like a teenager, fought like a lioness, danced like an angel, and her smile lit up whole rooms.

Call it The Light, The Power of The Universe, or as Mimi simply calls it: God… this is what has been Mimi's guiding force throughout her life. I would like to note that it has been a pleasure and an honour to serve as her Guardian Angel.

Breath of fresh air
One of Mimi's loyal readers called her a breath of fresh air and this describes her to a T. I'm looking forward to spending more time with her after my holidays.

If I had to sum her up in a few words, I would say that Mimi was one of a kind, and she will be remembered with great affection by family and friends, her readers, and even by those who merely had the briefest encounter with her, for her generosity, smile, and warm and kind heart.

Mimi's Guardian Angel
As written by family members, friends, & Mimi Emmanuel

LYRICAL POEM BY CRYSTAL

As a P.S. I attach a lyrical poem which I unearthed that was written by Mimi's youngest daughter, Crystal, at age 17 for the occasion of her Mum's 50th birthday, a year or so before her last medical emergency.

HAPPY 50th Birthday Mum

Dear Mum
on your 50th birthday Yoo hoo
Happy Birthday to you!

You are the best mum I could ever have and the nicest person know.

I have learned a lot about you lately and I think you're a bit like a butterfly precious necessary dainty beautiful delicate and been thru a lot and come out the better

bit like an eagle you really know how to make a nest and always see the bigger picture

A bit like a dolphin powerful smart intelligent brainy and have a calming effect and are great to have fun with and have that smile.

A bit like a Platypus very graceful with some extra sense that we don't have

Bit like a tiger your paws are soft but still theirs claws to protect your young and your stripes are like no one else's

Bit like a hippo your solid strong and have great tools in your mouth

Bit like an elephant which must have the biggest hart and is ever loyal even when it's not doing you much good

Like a swan elegant and a great leader

Tiny bit like a turtle tortoise they have a tough childhood and live real long have a strong protective shell that's very valuable and a cruisy personality

A little bit like a beaver forward thinking can get their teeth thru anything and hardworking always living on the edge

Little like a squirrel fast thoroughly determined to get your acorn totally gorgeous and great problem solving and always got their teeth in something

Bit like a bear warm and fuzzy great to hug and won't stand for anything that's not just.

But most of all you're like you and that's the way I like it I pray that the blessings of the Lord will follow you all the days of your life and that you may have peace victory and joy wherever you go.

Happy birthday Mum

Crystal

When the times comes, I think this heartfelt letter from Mimi's youngest would be hard to beat as 'Best Eulogy Ever Written.'

Can we take Mimi's eulogy-to-be at face value?

Is all that's written up in Mimi's eulogy-to-be genuine? Now, now, let's not get arguing with guardian angels.
Yes, it is imprinted in her heart. Many of the events took place already. Loving relationships are always a work in progress. The slacklining and jogging are on the to-do list, the *Letters to my Godson* are to be published soon, and the grandkids and last partner are, God willing, on the horizon. The inside garden is in process with basil, coriander, and sweet peas growing extremely well inside on the kitchen bench.

The secret of reverse engineering

The secret of reverse engineering lies in manifesting the desired, by stating and believing it to be so, *before* it has happened in 'real life.' Anything is possible, when you combine this mindset with prayers and positive actions.

In Mimi's life, prayers work miracles, and time will tell about living to a ripe old age with health completely restored.

The impossible can be brought about quite quickly, miracles may take a little longer.

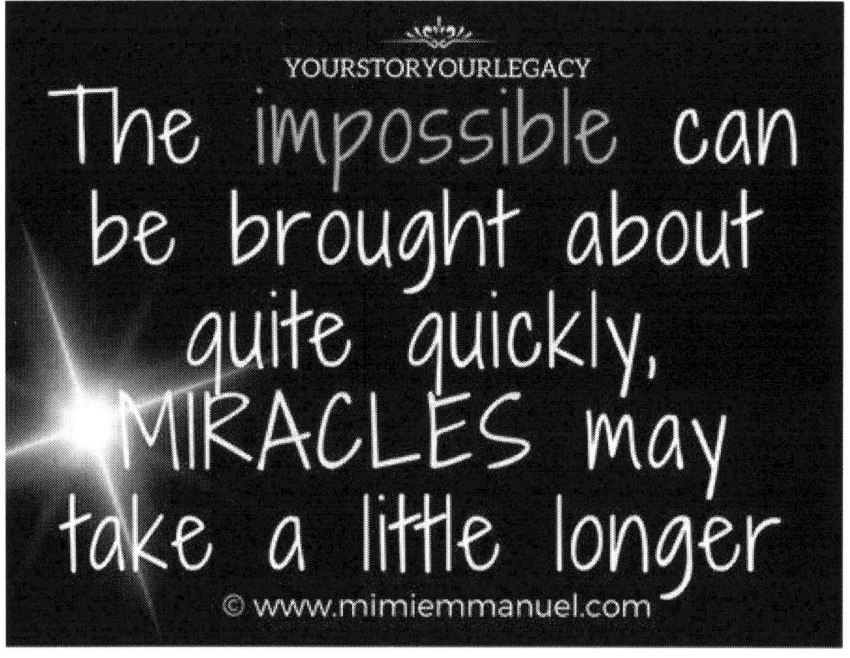

Crystal's letter was true for her when she wrote it, and is today treasured as much as it was on Mimi's birthday.

Why and how write your own eulogy-to-be?

Why would anyone want to write their own eulogy-to-be?

Lonnie asked her husband to start writing his eulogy. She said that, at his funeral, if he were to pass on first, she would be too sad to be able to say anything, and also, she did not know half the things that he had gotten up to and were worth mentioning.

That would be a good reason to write your own eulogy-to-be.

Mimi started writing her eulogy-to-be as she was recovering from life-threatening medical emergencies. She did this to get perspective on her life.

It sure gave her perspective, and she decided to create a life that matched her eulogy-to-be.

Some people write a bucket list. A eulogy-to-be is quite different. People usually write a bucket list of things that they would like to do in their lifetime. This list is supposed to keep them on track and inspire them to save up for this trip overseas and these fun things to do, and so on.

Your average eulogy is different in that most people are not remembered so much by the fun things they did or where they travelled, but more by what kind of person they were and how they made others feel.

Think about it.

> *Auntie Karen always polished the furniture every last Saturday of the month. She had a huge scrapbook collection. She followed the most popular celebrities on Twitter and had a following of 1200 Twitter 'friends.' She travelled to many different places, and every holiday she struck two items off her bucket list and then posted the events to her Facebook 'friends.'*

versus

> *Auntie Karen had a heart of gold. Many of the neighbourhood kids popped in after school to have a debrief and a slice of her famed banana bread. She tirelessly volunteered for the local UNICEF branch and throughout her life fostered children who affectionately called her Auntie Cuddles.*

What will you be remembered by?
Does it matter... to you?

I suggest that you write your eulogy-to-be with the help of friends and family.
For mature people, this can be a fun exercise as a group therapy kind of a thing. Get together with a couple of your besties and dream and design the rest of your life to your heart's desire.
For younger people, I suggest that parents facilitate and participate. Keep in mind that your story creates a legacy and what would you like it to be?

If you're happy with what you come up with, it is time to celebrate. Bring out the bubbly and toast the Good Forces that helped bring about a life well lived and worth celebrating.

If you're not happy with your eulogy-to-be as it stands right now, there is hope. Mimi wasn't happy either, and rewrote her eulogy-to-be so that it would match the life she'd be proud to live, and then took the first step in that direction.

In a short period of time she founded a place that sends blessings and inspirational messages out into the world called www.freescripturecards.com and www.mosaichouse.co. After creating MOSAIC HOUSE, so far Mimi has written 5 books and you can find these on Amazon at

www.amazon.com/author/mimiemmanuel.
Her books are on health and healing, and to help authors create the best possible legacy.

Live forever
Mimi believes in living forever, but even if you don't believe in an afterlife, you will still leave an imprint and live forever in the hearts of your loved ones.

> YOURSTORYOURLEGACY
> Those we LOVE never go away
> They live in our ♥ always
> © www.mimiemmanuel.com

The following is quoted from Tony Judt, historian, (02/91/1948-06/08/2010).

Just months before the historian Tony Judt died of ALS in 2010, he gave an interview to Terry Gross on NPR's Fresh Air. When she asked him about his spiritual beliefs, he replied as follows.

> *I don't believe in an afterlife. I don't believe in a single or multiple godhead. I respect people who do, but I don't believe it myself. But there's a big "but" which enters in here: I am much more conscious than I ever was, for obvious reasons, of what it will mean to people left behind once I'm dead.*
>
> *It won't mean anything for me, but it will mean a lot to them, and it's important for them, by which I mean my children or my wife or my close friends, that some spirit of me is, in a positive way, present in their lives, in their heads, in their imaginings, and so on.*
>
> *In one curious way I've come to believe in the afterlife as a place where I still have moral responsibilities, just as I do in this life, except that I can only exercise them before I get there. Once I get there, it'll be too late.*
>
> *So no god, no organized religion, but a developing sense that there's something bigger than the world we live in, including after we die, and that we have responsibilities in that world.*

Religion does not have to come into it. As Tony Judt puts it so eloquently, we're all responsible for the impact we have on the people around us.

Few, if any, of our Facebook or Twitter friends will be at our death bed, or care either way. How will we be remembered by our close friends and family members? How did we or do we impact their lives on a daily basis?

What unique task were we given and how did we live up to this?

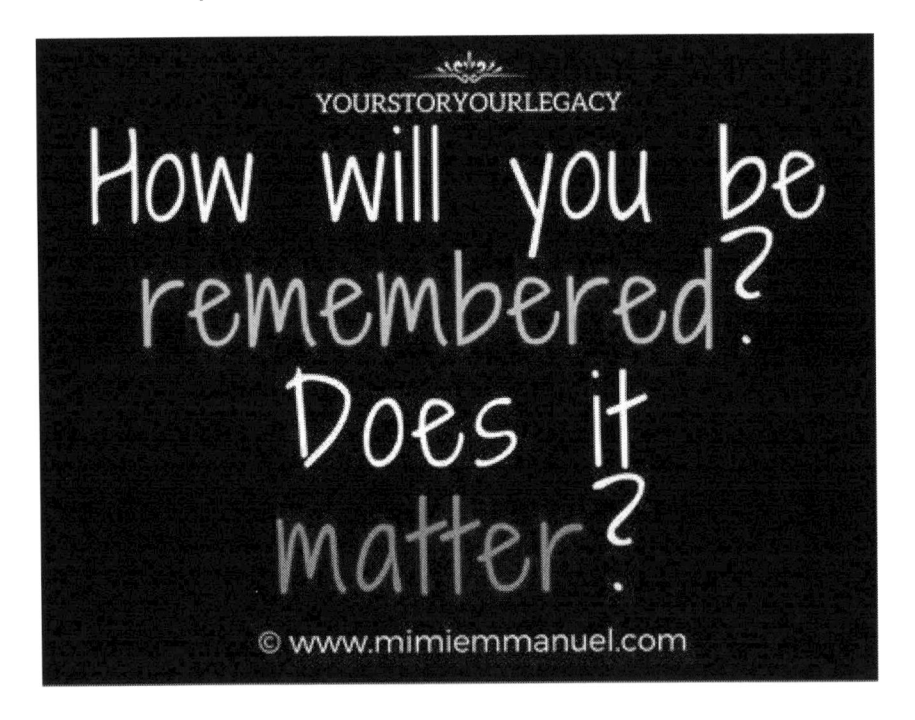

> YOURSTORYOURLEGACY
> **How will you be remembered? Does it matter?**
> © www.mimiemmanuel.com

Mimi decided that she wants to celebrate every single day of her life. At the end of her life as she knows it, others can continue the party, but at least she'll have started the celebrations and enjoyed it herself too, before she'll bow out and move into a different realm.

For help figuring out where to go from here, how to celebrate your life every single day, and make your legacy the best it can be, you can download Mimi's inspirational quotes collection from her website mimiemmanuel.com (in process). Or from www.freescripturecards.com on the following page you can download POPCORN FOR THE SOUL sayings http://liveforeverhowto.net/index.php/pages/gallery_present/?&per_page=16 to help keep you on track. Or tune in to her [YouTube channel.](YouTube channel) www.youtube.com/channel/UCl0WgXZ96EYQa_R5NlVQn2w

YOURSTORYOURLEGACY

Make every moment count

© www.mimiemmanuel.com

If you need help writing your own eulogy-to-be, you can use Mimi's as a guide, or download your own template from www.mimiemmanuel.com/downloads/template-for-eulogy-to-be

Check out the links provided under NOTES at the end of this book or contact Mimi on https://clarity.fm/memmanuel

AFTERWORD

Following are two end-of-life scenarios.
The first one is about Mary.

> Mary worked hard and faithfully paid her funeral insurance every week. Over a period of 64 years this came to a grand total of $53,000 of down payments.
> The funeral parlour did a magnificent job. The wreath of lilies was of medium size, with the heavy scent striking the mourners the moment they walked into the crematorium.
> Mary's was a traditional funeral with black hearse and black coffin, followed by mourners dressed in black with memories rolling off their cheeks.
> The subdued faces of the professionally engaged pallbearers added to the sad and dignified ceremony.
> The priest read out Mary's eulogy, and tea and cakes were served in the function room.
> Afterwards everyone said that it was a beautiful funeral.

The second one is about Maria.

Maria also worked hard and never managed to put any money aside for her burial.

When the time came, all her friends pitched in. A mattress was placed under the coffin to ensure a soft ride in the trailer, which was wonderfully decorated with wild flowers. Petals blowing in the breeze teased the procession following.

Everyone that came to celebrate Maria's life was dressed in white, with colourful scarves, carrying bouquets of daisies and roses.

Tears of laughter ran down the cheeks of all those that came to celebrate Maria's life as they recalled her mischievous tricks and colourful life.

Everyone agreed that this was the best celebration of life they ever attended.

There is a huge difference between the two end-of-life scenarios. One is of mourning whilst the other is one of celebration. Neither one is better or worse than the other. Both are appropriate and chosen specifically for the person who is being farewelled.

Which end of life scenario resonates with you? What are you planning for?
Some people have a funeral first and plan for a memorial service or Celebration-of-Life-Get-Together, after.

Whatever you choose when you're living and celebrating your life, be sure that it reflects you.

Mimi's grandpa always said that he would like to die in his sleep, and at age 74, he did just that. Peacefully in his old grandpa chair, he passed on whilst he was asleep.

There are Biblical accounts of how some people did not die. For instance, 'God took Enoch' and the prophet Elisha witnessed his teacher Elijah being carried into heaven in a chariot of fire with horses of fire.
A number of witnesses described seeing how Jesus was lifted up into heaven till a cloud hid Him from their sight.

In closing, I remember a story about three laughing monks who travelled from town to town. Their sole mission in life was to make people laugh. One died whilst they were traveling. His final wish was to be cremated in his kimono without washing his body. His friends complied, and when they set him afire, the fireworks hid into his clothing burst into a spectacular finale. He died the way he had lived, making people laugh.

YOUR STORY IS YOUR LEGACY

Your story creates a legacy. Most of us don't reflect much on life, nor death, because we're so caught up in the daily hustle and bustle. It is good to stop every now and then and realise that we have a fair amount of control over the legacy we would like to leave behind.

Dr. R. Covey, author of *The 7 Habits of Highly Effective People* says under Habit 1: Be Proactive. "*Your life doesn't just 'happen.' Whether you know it or not, it is carefully designed by you. The choices, after all, are yours. You choose happiness. You choose sadness. You choose decisiveness. You choose ambivalence. You choose success. You choose failure. You choose courage. You choose fear. Just remember that every moment, every situation, provides a new choice. And in doing so, it gives you a perfect opportunity to do things differently to produce more positive results.*"

I think what Dr. Covey is saying here is that we are not defined by the events in our life, but we are defined by how we choose to respond to life's curve balls.

What would you like people say about you when you're gone? Now go and live up to that. In the words of Ian's Auntie, *"Life's too short for tepid food and tepid people."*

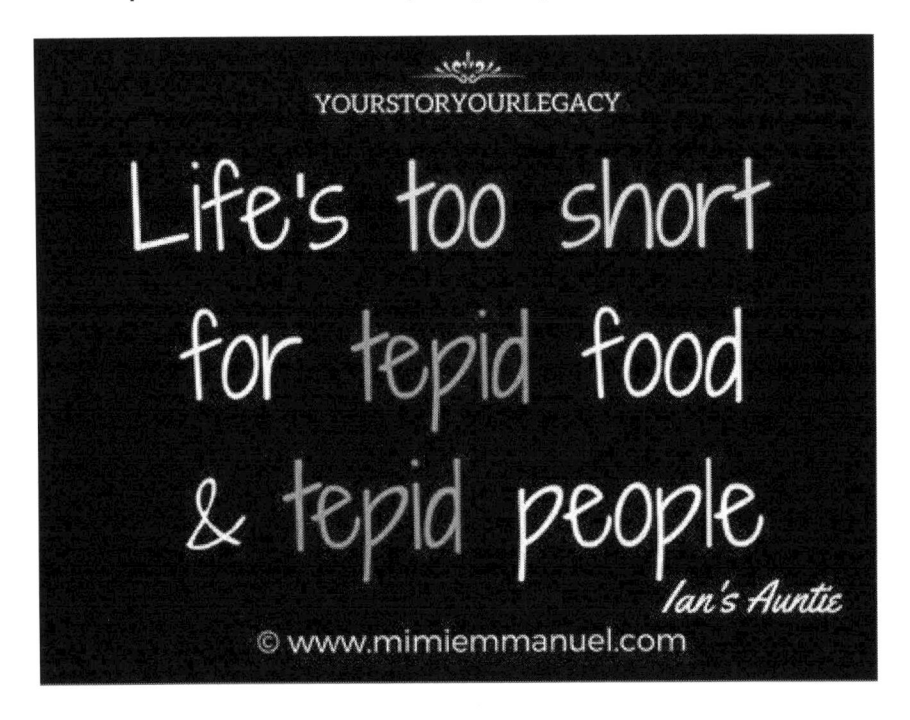

> **YOURSTORYOURLEGACY**
>
> Life's too short for tepid food & tepid people
>
> *Ian's Auntie*
>
> © www.mimiemmanuel.com

If this short book made you think about your life and how happy you are about the direction it is going, it has done its job.

Thank you for your review

If you liked what you read, please consider leaving a review on Amazon by Googling 'Mimi Emmanuel legacy.' Your review will make it easier for other readers to find this book.

You can sign up here
http://eepurl.com/bHUzf5
to be informed of Mimi's upcoming books and receive the occasional freebie.

Mimi's books combined have become #1 bestsellers in more than 43 categories. You can find her books on Amazon and www.mimiemmanuel.com.

My Story of Survival
Mimi's Book Launch Plan
God Healed Me
Journal for God Healed Me
The Holy Grail of Book Launching
Live Your Best Life
Anthologies I contributed to are:
Glimpses of Light and
Like a Girl.

Coming up: "*Letters to my Godson.*"

TEMPLATE FOR EULOGY-TO-BE

Remember, we're writing here for the living, not for those who are not with us any longer. We are writing to achieve the most awesome life possible and making your story the best it can be, leaving an amazing legacy. You can download your own template from www.mimiemmanuel.com/downloads/template-for-eulogy-to-be

How do we reverse engineer our life?

By speaking out blessings over our life instead of curses.

You don't like your boss and he doesn't like you?

Don't go around complaining.

Make your eulogy to-be say something to the effect, that you had a wonderful relationship with all employers and added value wherever you went.

Your mother in law is not keen on you and sets you up for failure? It's a common situation.

Why don't you refer to her as your bestie in your eulogy to-be and praise her cooking skills? Then you casually leave those notes laying around for her to read.

Your children won't behave?

Express 'what you want,' *not* 'what is' in your eulogy to-be. Note that you relished all time spent with your children and their exemplary behaviour, particularly in stressful situations.

How does this work? It just does. It opens your mindset to other possibilities that are preferable over what you have. Then your subconscious mind sets out to create what you've put in writing as if it's already a reality.

If you don't believe me, you'll have to try it out for yourself and see what happens.

What have you got to lose?

1. Introduction
Who is giving the speech on behalf of who?

In Mimi's case, her Guardian Angel piped up. Someone else may have a family member, their puppy, or parrot speak on their behalf.

2. Childhood
Fill in with funny memories, people, and places.

If your parents weren't hands-on and left you to your own devices, you may say something to the effect of, 'My childhood left me with wonderful opportunities to explore life and become self-reliant.'

Remember what you loved doing as a child... is this still the case? Did you fulfil those child hood dreams?

3. Schooling and Education

Mention memorable events and consider if there are gaps in your education that you would like to fill in. You can write these qualifications in your eulogy-to-be. Yes, you can, you have my permission. Now plan on how to make this happen!

4. Work and Professional

This is where you can get the red pen out and scrap all the bits you do not like and replace these with what you would like to see happen in your life. You may have heard about the 3-book rule of becoming an expert? It is never too late to become an expert in your chosen field of expertise.

www.siamohajer.com/the-3-book-rule-of-being-an-expert/

What is it that you have always wanted to be or do? BE and DO! It is never too late nor too early to get going on this!

5. Family and Marriage

Are you single and would like to be married? This is where you can meet your soul-mate. You can even tell the story of how you met. You'll be surprised to find out how Higher Powers, the Universe, and Angels listen to intent and help bring your deepest desires about.

A little testy with the in-laws? Make your mother-in-law your bestie in your eulogy-to-be and watch the miracles unfold.

6. Voluntary work, hobbies, and sport

You can admit it and I promise I won't tell anyone. You've always wanted to be a champion axe thrower, haven't you? There will be a club somewhere whose members will love to help you achieve that dream.

If overseas is beckoning for schools to be built and water pumps to be installed, you can plan your holidays around this, and bring it about.

If you're young and clumsy, but willing to contribute, you can offer to walk the neighbour's dog and pull out their garbage bin.

If you're old, on a pension, and confined to bed, you can donate $1/week to a good cause. That is 52 dollars, each year of your good money making a difference in the world, and for instance, feeding 700 children that otherwise would go without.

https://feedthehungry.org.au. It is never too late for noble deeds and childhood dreams.

7. Friends, Family, and Colleagues

Did anyone ever say anything nice about you? Insert this into your eulogy-to-be. And if they didn't... ask them about your best qualities and add this in. Bask for a moment in that wonderful feeling of being appreciated. Why wait till it is too late?

We can all learn from the Dutch Funeral Insurance Company Dela who literally moved a whole nation to share the love around whilst people are still alive. The media Grand Prix was awarded to this small Dutch funeral-insurance company for encouraging people to say something wonderful about the people they care about while they're still around to hear it. See link under NOTES.

8. Look around you

Look around you and see where you can uniquely contribute your skills and talents. For instance, I am the only Godmother of my Godchild and therefore uniquely placed to contribute to his life spiritually and otherwise as only a Godmother can do. The same for my children and so on.

How are you uniquely positioned to contribute in ways that only you can?

It is likely to be right in front of you. It is likely to be challenging and chances are that you are the only person placed in this position. This is where you can shine.

9. For Inspiration

For inspiration I suggest that you look up the following eulogies; The Rev. Mychal Judge by the Rev. Michael Duffy, Mahatma Mohandas Gandhi's Funeral Eulogy by Jawaharlal Nehru,

Diana Spencer Princess of Wales' Eulogy as presented by her brother Charles Spencer, 9th Earl Spencer Space Shuttle Challenger Crew by Ronald Reagan, Rosa Parks by Oprah Winfrey, Steve Irwin by Bindi Irwin, Steve Jobs by Mona Simpson, The Rev. Clementa Pinckney by President Barack Obama, Graham Chapman by John Cleese, Lorna Colbert by Stephen Colbert and Richard Nixon by Bill Clinton.

10. Reflections, Dreams, Hopes

This is where you give it all you've got. The sky is the limit here. What do you want to achieve in life, with your family, for society?

How can you best apply your skills, and contribute in the most meaningful way, whilst enjoying living your best possible story and leaving your best possible legacy?

What words would you like people to use when they describe you? Warm-hearted, generous, kind, helpful, funny, entrepreneurial? Make it happen.

If you like music, you can add your favourite tune here, or your favourite theatre play that fits in with the theme of your life as you intend for it to unfold. I'll go with "Chariots of Fire" by Vangelis, what about you?

11. Go for it! Make it happen!
Today take the first step towards living your best life possible!

Just one step is all it takes and you're on your way.

NOTES

Made in HIS image... by the breath of HIS mouth
www.biblegateway.com/passage/?search=Psalm+33%3A6%2C+Genesis+1%3A27&version=KJV

Eulogy writer Ian Heydon
www.eulogywriter.com.au/self_eulogy.html

Must read: *The 7 Habits of Highly Effective People*
www.stephencovey.com/7habits/7habits.php

Sample eulogies:
www.whiteladyfunerals.com.au/arranging-funeral/how-to-write-a-eulogy

Dutch Funeral Insurance Company Dela raises the bar:
http://adage.com/article/special-report-cannes-2013/netherlands-dela-wins-top-media-prize-cannes/242186/

More sample eulogies:
www.write-out-loud.com/free-sample-eulogies.html

www.eulogyspeech.net/sample-eulogy/#.WYZwS4iGNik

Ten greatest eulogies of all time:
https://northumbriancountdown.wordpress.com/2012/08/19/10-greatest-eulogies-of-all-time/

Chariots of Fire by Vangelis
www.youtube.com/watch?v=CSav51fVlKU

Inspirational Eulogies
www.legacy.com/news/advice-and-support/article/nine-best-eulogies

www.funeralwise.com/plan/eulogy/famous_overview/

Remember also when the times comes, this heartfelt letter from Mimi's youngest, Crystal. It sure would be hard to beat as 'Best Eulogy Ever Written.'

Mimi's root vegetable soup recipe
Boil one medium beetroot, one small onion, two very large carrots and a decent slice of pumpkin together with pepper and salt or

seasoning of your choice in a soup maker or saucepan.
Heat, blend, serve with a slice of toast and a dollop of sour cream. Enjoy!

Upcoming New Release

Letters to My Godson

This is a devotional work of fiction dedicated to my Godchild.

This book is the perfect gift idea for Godparents as well as Grandparents who take the spiritual education of their God- and grandchildren seriously.

Most of us have heard the expression that it takes a village to raise a child. As Lewis' Godmother, Mimi is keen to do the right thing by her Godson, and as a feisty woman with plenty of opinions of her own she mobilises the village and invites her Godson's Mum and Dad and grandparents, and also her friends, to help provide her Godson Lewis with a balanced view on all things God, according to their culture and family history.

Letters to my Godson are the letters written by a Godmother to her Godson when she was not able to visit him due to distance.

Is God real?

Let's find out.

Thank you for leaving a review on Amazon if you enjoyed *Live Your Best Life by writing your own eulogy.*

You can sign up at http://eepurl.com/bHUzf5 to be informed of Mimi's upcoming books and receive the occasional freebie

©www.mimiemmanuel.com

Printed in Great Britain
by Amazon